Deer

This book describes the different kinds of deer across the world—the Red, Fallow and Roe Deer in Britain; the Reindeer and Elk of Europe and Asia; the Wapiti, Moose and Caribou in America; and the Hog and Swamp Deer of the tropics.

The author gives the deer's calendar: the "rutting" or mating season, the birth of fawns and how they grow up, and the annual shedding and regrowing of antlers. He explains their behaviour and seasonal activities, their keen sense of smell and hearing, and how they camouflage themselves and warn others of danger. And he tells the story of their survival in a changing world—sometimes hunted, sometimes protected, sometimes both.

There are more than 50 illustrations and the book contains a glossary, a section on where to find out more, a reading list and an index.

Deer

Ralph Whitlock

Priory Press Limited

Young Naturalist Books

Foxes
Squirrels
Bats
Rabbits and Hares
Hedgehogs
Frogs and Toads
Snakes and Lizards
Badgers
Deer
Spiders
Otters
Rats and Mice
Stoats and Weasels
Bees and Wasps
Ants
Beetles
Birds of Prey
Pond Life
Crickets and Grasshoppers

SBN 85078 181 7
Copyright © 1974 Priory Press Ltd
2nd impression, 1976
First published in 1974
by Priory Press Ltd
49, Lansdowne Place, Hove, Sussex BN3 1HS
Filmset by Keyspools Ltd, Golborne, Lancs
Printed in Great Britain at
The Pitman Press, Bath

Contents

1 : What Deer are Like

Although there are deer scattered over most parts of Britain, Europe and North America, you do not see them very often. They remain hidden away in woods and forests and on mountain sides. For this reason they seem rather mysterious creatures.

The most noticeable things about deer are their horns or antlers. With most kinds of deer only the males, or *stags*, have them. They are branched, like the branches of a tree, with sharp tips at the ends.

An odd thing about the antlers is that they are shed every year. Usually they drop off in the spring. Soon afterwards a new set of antlers starts to grow and is complete by autumn. Each new set is bigger and more branched than the previous one, until the stag reaches the age of six or seven years, after which they usually get no bigger. Often the deer eats the old set when it is shed!

Deer are *herbivorous* animals, which means that they eat plants. Like cows, they are *ruminants*; they have more than one stomach and when they find plenty of food they eat as much as possible quickly, storing it in one stomach

7

Left: A red deer hart or stag of ten, with ten points on his magnificent antlers.

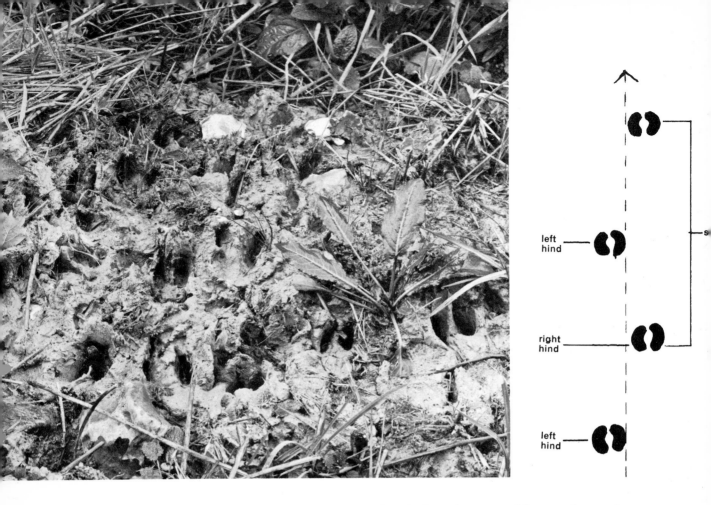

Above: The tracks or *slots* of red deer in a muddy patch, and *(right)* the prints of a walking reindeer.

without bothering to digest it. Then they sit down in some quiet place, bring back the undigested greenstuff into their mouth, chew it and pass it down to another stomach. This known as chewing the cud. We may often see cows doing it as they sit in a meadow. Deer do exactly the same.

Deer are cloven-hoofed animals. They have horny hooves, cleft or split in the middle like a cow's or a sheep's. You can often see their tracks, or hoofprints, in the mud or snow when the animals themselves are hidden.

Deer range in size from the Moose, which is a giant, to small forest deer, which are not much bigger than hares. Most of them, however, are rather large.

Most deer live in forests and park-like country rather than on grassy plains; but there are some, like the Reindeer and Caribou, which roam over the icy plains, known as the tundra, on the margin of the Arctic Ocean.

Seven kinds of deer roam wild in Britain, and many

A small herd of roe deer tries to scrape some food from a frozen field.

others may be seen, more or less free, in parks. Of the seven, four have been brought into the country and turned loose only in recent times. They are the Chinese Water Deer, the Muntjac, the Sika and the Reindeer. They live in only a few places in Britain.

The other three deer, which have been in Britain for a long time, are the Red Deer, the Fallow Deer and the Roe Deer. Of these the fallow deer is not a native, having been introduced from southern Europe. It has, however, been here for so long that in many districts it is the commonest of the three. It is said to have been first brought into the country by the Romans.

The red deer is found throughout Europe, except in some of the Mediterranean countries. It is really a forest animal, though in Britain it is found in greatest numbers on the Scottish mountains. These mountain animals tend to be smaller than those which live in the forests, probably because there is less food and the climate is harsher. In England red deer live in suitable forest regions, as far south as the New Forest and Exmoor.

The roe deer, which is a small animal about the size of a goat, also lives in forests. At one time it was extinct in all except the northern counties of England and in Scotland. About 150 years ago, however, landowners began to bring them back and turn them loose in woods in southern England, especially in Dorset. Now they have become common again.

A young red deer stag. His antlers tell us that he is a *brocket*, less than two years old.

A roe deer buck. His antlers are smaller but sharper.

A fallow deer buck with his antlers almost full grown but in "velvet"—covered with a soft downy skin.

Newborn Chinese water deer, only 9 inches tall, at Whipsnade Zoo.

The fallow deer is another woodland animal, as are most of the kinds of deer which have been brought into the country. The Chinese water deer and the muntjac are both small deer, even smaller than the roe deer. Muntjacs are often less than eighteen inches high. They live in dense woods and you very rarely see them.

The Sika, or Japanese deer, is much larger. It is a

Reindeer feeding on moss. They also eat lichen, shoots, leaves and bark.

relation of the red deer, though not quite as large. It has settled down and become quite common in south-east England.

Only one herd of reindeer lives in Britain. They were turned loose on the tops of the Cairngorm mountains in Scotland about twenty years ago and are still there, although their numbers do not seem to be increasing. Probably the climate is not quite cold enough for them.

In prehistoric times two kinds of elk, or moose, lived in the British Isles. One was the Irish Elk, a huge animal whose antlers alone weighed 80 – 90 pounds. It became extinct long ago. The other, the European Elk, still lives in forests in northern Europe and Asia and was to be found in Scotland until about 1300 A.D. However, it no longer lives there now.

Right: An elk calf a few days old, born in Helsinki Zoo, is watched over by its four-year-old mother.

2 : The Red Deer

The red deer is the largest surviving British animal. Like the elk, the bear, the wild ox and other big animals, it would have been killed off long ago if people had not so much enjoyed hunting it. In many European countries as well as Britain the red deer was, for hundreds of years, regarded as an important animal which could be hunted and killed only by the king or high-ranking nobles. Ordinary people were forbidden to kill or even chase a deer, under penalty of death or imprisonment.

The red deer lived in the forest, but the word "forest" did not in those days necessarily mean woodland. It referred to any expanse of waste or uncultivated land. The New Forest in Hampshire was such an area. William the Conqueror made a law decreeing that it was a royal forest reserved for deer, which only he and his courtiers could hunt. At one time over eighty royal forests existed in England.

Gentry in the Middle Ages spent much of their time, when they were not at war, hunting deer, and so became very familiar with them. They gave special names to the

Left : A red deer hind. She has no antlers, and so defends herself and her young with powerful kicks of her hooves.

A first year male calf or knobber, in velvet.

deer at different stages of their life. Female deer were, and are, known as *hinds*; and young deer as *calves*. Male deer are nowadays known as stags, but the name properly refers only to a mature male, after he is five years old.

In the first year of his life a male deer calf is known as a *knobber*, because he has two knobs on the front of his head, where his horns will grow. In the second year, small spikes, or points, develop from these knobs, and the deer is known as a *brocket*. In the third year the first branch appears in the antlers, and the young deer is then a *spayad*. In the fourth year he develops two forward antlers and a branch near the tip of his main horn. He is now a *staggard*. In the fifth year he grows more points on

Below left : A drawing showing how red deer antlers grow. The large antler is of a stag in its fifth year.
Right : A brocket.

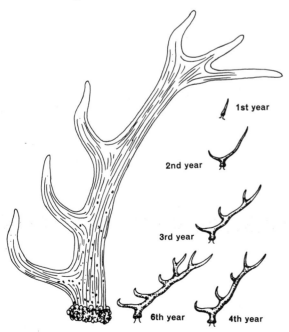

1st year

2nd year

3rd year

6th year   4th year

his antler and becomes a full-grown *stag*. Later, though not necessarily in the next year, he grows more points to his antlers, and when he has ten he is known as a *hart* or *stag of ten*. He may grow even more, and when he has twelve or more points he is a *stag royal*.

In the Middle Ages the term *stag royal* also meant a stag which had been hunted by the king and had, by its skill or endurance, managed to escape. It was thereafter held in high regard and reigned as a kind of king in its forest for many years. Fifteen to eighteen years is said to be the normal span of life for red deer, but people think that some live even longer.

A red deer stag weighs about 200 pounds, though some are heavier. They stand about four feet high at the shoulder. The long, branched antlers of an adult male measure between three and four feet from its brow to the tip of its antlers.

The red deer is reddish-brown, with a patch of light brown hair around its short tail. Full-grown stags have manes, which are longest and thickest in autumn, the mating season. In winter their coats fade to a brownish grey.

The females, or hinds, are smaller and less brightly coloured. They have no horns.

For the first month or so of their lives, red deer calves are spotted with white, and their coats are soft and woolly. The spots fade and have disappeared by the time the

The spots of the red deer calves make them hard to see in a dappled, sunlit wood.

calves are eight weeks old. The spots are thought to be a form of camouflage. They are like spots of sunlight shining through forest trees and so help to protect the baby calves by making them difficult to see when they are lying snug among the ferns.

A few stags fail to produce horns. They are known as *hummels* and are often bigger and heavier than normal stags.

The senses of the red deer are very keen. The animals are always alert and can detect danger by sight, smell and sound. Like most kinds of deer, they have large ears.

Their antlers are curious things. After they fall off in April, the knobs from which they sprang are covered with soft skin and hair, known as *velvet*. When the new antlers

Two stags interlock their horns and fight for their harems.

start to grow in May, the velvet grows with them and covers them throughout the summer. In autumn, as the mating season approaches, it shrivels and peels off, leaving the bare bone of the antlers exposed. A stag will often rub its antlers against a tree to get rid of the velvet once it has started to peel.

The antlers are used in two ways. One is to fight with other stags in the mating season. The other is to do battle with enemies which might harm the stag or his family.

When he is fighting with rival stags the red deer stag seldom uses the points of his antlers. The branches are so arranged that they interlock, and so the battle takes the

Above: A stag in autumn, with the velvet half peeled off his antlers. *Below:* A fine stag of ten, with the velvet gone and the hard bone of the antlers revealed.

form of fitting their antlers together and pushing. The strongest, who pushes hardest, wins. The loser is seldom hurt. He breaks loose and runs away.

It is different when the stag is defending himself or his hinds against other attackers such as wolves. Then it does use the points of his antlers, and they are highly effective. A stag in the mating season is a very dangerous animal, which is quite prepared to attack, and if possible kill, a human being. No-one should go anywhere near it.

The red deer is polygamous, which means that a stag will have a number of wives. The strongest stag, which can chase its rivals away, naturally collects most wives. Curiously, hummels often collect a harem of wives. Although they have no horns they are, as we have seen, often larger and heavier than ordinary stags, and so their weight helps them win their mating battles.

Probably they are larger and heavier because they do not have to grow antlers. Growing these horns each spring puts a great strain on the body of the ordinary stag. In particular, he needs lots of calcium and other minerals to produce the bones of the antlers. It is in places where there are few minerals like these that the stags most often eat their antlers when they shed them.

3 : The Calendar of the Red Deer

The red deer is a sociable animal. All through the summer it lives in herds, the two sexes in separate herds. The herds of hinds, or females, are often larger than those of the stags, because the hinds have their calves with them, and so they stick close together for defence. The young stags usually remain with the hind herds until their third year.

A red deer stag wallows in a muddy pool, trying to keep the flies off.

The hinds are always on the alert for danger, and when one senses it she raises the alarm by uttering a sharp bark. The stag herd seem to stay together for company, not safety, and often one of the older and more experienced stags will wander off on his own.

Herds of deer have territories which they roam over, seldom going outside the limits. The summer territories and the winter territories are, however, usually different. In Scotland the deer spend the summer on the moors and mountains, but they retire to the forests in winter.

Stags, as we have already seen, shed their antlers in April. Through the summer new antlers are growing. The stags try to keep out of sight, because without their antlers it is harder for them to defend themselves. By August the new antlers are complete, and the stags are rubbing off the covering of velvet. By September the antlers are bare, and the stag herds are beginning to break up.

The mating, or *rutting*, season begins at the end of September and lasts for about six weeks. A big stag, leaving his herd behind, will go wandering across country, seeking a herd of hinds.

While he is searching for his wives, or *harem*, he is a splendid and formidable animal, with a new pair of antlers and a shaggy mane. At this time of year he loves to wallow in peat bogs, probably because he is irritated by flies, so that his coat often looks black rather than red. At other times of the year he is a silent animal, apart from a few

A herd of stags near Balmoral in Scotland. They have come down to the woods and valleys for winter, but still find it hard to get enough to eat.

grunts, but now he develops a mighty voice. He struts about roaring, or *belling*, as it is called, to keep his hinds together and also to challenge any other males.

After about six weeks of this, the stag retires and drops into his winter habits in a stag herd. His voice disappears and his lighter winter coat begins to grow.

For the hind herds, life goes on much as usual. The herd did not break up while mating was going on, the younger males and females who were not old enough to breed still hanging around. As for the calves of the past season, they continue to suck their mothers throughout the rutting season. Indeed, many of them seem to do so throughout the following winter and until just before the next crop of calves is born.

The *gestation* period, or time between mating and the birth of the calves, is 230 – 240 days. The calves are therefore mostly born in May and June. Each hind has one calf.

Just before calving the hind leaves the herd and finds a quiet spot, ideally in a woodland glade with plenty of ferns. The baby deer is a lovely little creature, with violet eyes and a coat dappled with white. It can stand and even run soon after birth, but it much prefers to lie quietly in its nest of grass and fern for a week or two. Then its mother takes it back to the herd.

The calf usually weighs about 14 pounds at birth. It takes two or three years to become fully grown. Both males

28

Right : A stag in the rutting season. His antlers are hard and strong, and he goes about roaring or *belling* loudly.

A stag chases his mate at the rut.

A red deer calf a few hours old. It can already stand and even run about.

A hind feeds her dappled, spotted youngster.

and females start to breed when they are three or four years old. Some hinds produce a calf every year, some one in two years.

Deer are *nocturnal* animals, which means that they usually come out to feed at night. In summer they spend the day sitting quietly in the heather on high hilltops,

33

Above : A red deer stag with part of his harem. *Right :* A young stag reaches up to eat the leaves of a tree.

where they can feel the breeze, for they have a lot of trouble with flies and other biting insects. In the evening twilight they rouse themselves and move downhill to the best feeding ground they can find. They also like a mud-bath in a bog or stream. In winter, of course, the flies which have pestered them have disappeared. Food, however, is scarce, and they need to spend most of their time searching for it.

Those which can still live in or on the edge of forests eat the leaves, twigs and sometimes the bark of the trees, as

34

well as the grass beneath them. Where the forests have been cleared and replaced by farmland the deer eat the farmer's crops of grain, roots and vegetables. They also feed on moss, lichens, berries and fungi. Red deer are not surprisingly unpopular with farmers and foresters.

Deer seem to have a sixth sense which warns them when bad weather is coming. Before a heavy snowfall they will come down from the higher ground to shelter in valleys and woods.

Winter is a hard time for deer. Although they have very few natural enemies in Britain, apart from man, about half the calves born die before they are grown up. The cause of death is usually stress or starvation caused by bad weather, and many young deer are drowned in floods.

Stags are probably at their best when they are about twelve or thirteen years old. After that they start to decline. Each new set of antlers is smaller and less branched, and in their fights to keep a harem in autumn they generally lose. They live till they are about seventeen years old.

4: The Fallow Deer

The fallow deer is smaller than the red deer, standing three feet high and weighing from 80 to 180 pounds. The male is much larger and heavier than the female, in some instance twice the size.

Young fallow deer bucks in velvet.

The Fallow Deer

Its colour is a yellowish brown or reddish brown, well dappled with white spots along the back and sides. These markings make excellent camouflage when the deer is standing still in a woodland glade, for the pattern is the same as that of beams of sunlight falling through the leaves of trees onto a carpet of ferns. The underparts are white, and so is the tail, which has a black "margin" round it. When the deer is startled and runs away, its tail stands up and the white patch stands out very clearly against the black, thus warning other deer of danger.

The fallow deer is a woodland animal. It lies sleeping or chewing the cud in thickets or glades during the day and comes out to feed in the late evening and early morn-

A fallow deer buck. Notice the flies buzzing round him, and the way his alert ears point forward.

A mixed herd of fallow deer.

ing, also on moonlit nights. It eats grass, leaves, roots and the farmer's crops. In parks, where the deer know they are in no danger, they often lie in the open by day and sometimes move about, feeding.

Fallow deer have very keen senses of smell and hearing. Their sight is not so acute, although still quite good. They are quick to detect movement, but they will sometimes fail to see a man who stands motionless and downwind, not many yards away.

The antlers of the fallow deer are different from the red deer's by being flatter. As with the red deer, they are shed in April. A new set, more elaborate than the previous one, grows during summer. Only the stag has them, and there

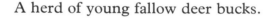

A herd of young fallow deer bucks.

are words to describe stags at various stages of antler development.

From the time the young stag starts to grow its antlers (which is around Christmas time, when it is nine months old) to the time of the first shedding the animal is known as a *pricket*. In its second year it is a *sorel*. Next year it becomes a *sore*. At four years old it is a *bare buck*. Over the next few years it grows into a *buck*, reaching maturity when it is about eight years old. Some bucks go on to grow larger and even more elaborate antlers until they are about twelve years old. These super bucks are known as *great bucks*.

Female fallow deer are known as *does*; young fallow deer as *fawns*.

For most of the year the females and males of the fallow deer are grouped in separate herds. After shedding his antlers in spring the male is very shy for a few months, and keeps hidden in the depths of the woods. By August his new set of antlers is complete and he starts to rub off the velvet, just as the red deer stag does.

Behaviour at mating time is, however, different from the red deer's. Instead of roaming around collecting wives, the fallow buck marks out a plot of land, known as a rutting stand, and lets the females come to him. The rutting stand is normally an area of about 60 yards by 40 in a forest clearing. The buck marks it by thrashing the nearby bushes and small trees with his antlers, by

A fallow buck charging a man. In the mating season they lose all fear and are very dangerous.

exuding a scent upon them (from glands under his eyes) and by pawing with his feet. Then he marches up and down, often for hours, groaning loudly and throwing up dirt with his feet. The does, some of them with their fawns, come to watch him, and mating duly takes place. Sometimes another buck appears and then, if the two are about equally matched, a tremendous fight takes place. Bucks do not often get killed in these spectacular battles, however.

41

The rutting season lasts throughout October. During this time the buck is very active and excited and eats very little, so that by November he is thin and tired. Like the red deer stag, at this season he is dangerous and seems to lose his fear of man. The does keep watch for signs of danger.

The gestation period is about eight months, so the fawns are born in spring, the same time as red deer. When the fawn is about to be born, the doe goes off to a quiet and well concealed place in dense thickets. She leaves her baby there, returning once or twice in the day or night to feed it. After a few days the fawn goes with her. They meet with other does and fawns and so form the beginning of a herd. The fawns stay with their mothers right through the summer and the following winter and are driven away in March, not long before the next is due to be born.

Fallow deer are most common in well wooded districts in southern England and are uncommon in Wales and most of Scotland. They prefer broad-leaved woodlands to conifers. A herd will live in the same area of forest for many years, each new generation following well marked tracks among the trees. Generations of stags, too, will use the same rutting stands.

Sometimes people see fallow deer which are black or white; these are usually bucks. Fallow deer normally live about ten years.

Right : A fallow buck in the snow.

5: The Roe Deer

Roe deer are different from both red and fallow deer in quite a number of ways. They are much smaller, standing only 2 to $2\frac{1}{2}$ feet high and weighing from 40 to 60 pounds. Their horns are short (usually only the male has them) and seldom have more than two short branches.

Left: Roe deer in the summer. *Below:* A roe buck and doe. Roe deer group in families rather than large herds.

A roe deer fawn. Its first coat is yellowish brown with white spots.

The roe deer is different in its habits, too. It does not form large herds but goes about, during most of the year, in family groups. A typical roe deer group consists of a buck, a doe and two fawns.

The rut, or mating season, is in July and August.

The rutting stand is a circular area, in which the buck chases the doe around some trees. At this season the bucks bark loudly, and the does answer them with a high-

A roe buck races for safety across the grass.

pitched cry. The roe buck may have several wives, but not a large harem like the red and fallow deer.

After mating, the bucks go away on their own for a month or two. They shed their antlers in November and December, and the new set, which they start to grow almost at once, is full grown by April.

A curious thing occurs in the breeding cycle of the roe deer. Although mating takes place in July or August, the growth of the baby deer within its mother's body does not begin till December. This is known as *delayed implantation*. The young are born in May or early June, and the doe usually produces twins.

In summer the roe deer has a foxy red coat with a white tail. In October it moults and gets its winter coat, which is usually dark brown or grey, with white marks on its throat but no white tail. This coat it loses in its second moult, in May. The young roe deer are speckled with white, much like fallow and red deer, and they keep this juvenile coat for a year.

Although the roe deer has antlers which look much less impressive than those of the fallow or red deer, fatal fights between males happen more often. This is because the short, sharp points on the horns act like daggers and are very dangerous. The roe buck, too, is a fierce animal in the mating season. As well as pawing the soil and scoring the trees around his rutting ring with his horns, he has a gland on his forehead which he uses to mark the boundaries of his domain, and he will immediately tackle any other buck who trespasses on it.

At all other times of the year, roe deer are very shy and secretive. They lurk in thickets, ditches and dense forest coverts. When disturbed they dart out and bound away, dodging this way and that. They come out to feed at night and are not often seen about, though they are, in fact, quite common in much of Britain.

6: The Sika, Muntjac and Other Deer

The sika, or Japanese deer, is, though smaller, very like the red deer in appearance and behaviour. Its coat is, however, spotted with white or yellow in summer, like that of the fallow deer, and it has a prominent white tail patch. In winter it is dark brown. Its antlers are smaller

A sika stag peeps curiously through the trees.

than the red deer's. Instead of roaring or *belling* in the mating season, the sika stag utters a whistling call. The rutting season takes place in August and September, and the calves are born in June.

Sika deer were brought to Britain from Japan about three hundred years ago and now live in woods in many parts of England, as well as in Ireland.

The muntjac is like the roe deer in size and behaviour. It is only 18 to 24 inches high, and its antlers are short, sharp but very little branched. Two of its teeth are developed into tusks, which it uses when it is fighting.

The muntjac does not gather in herds but wanders either alone or in pairs in the forest. In India, China and Indo-China, where its native home is, it lurks in thick undergrowth in jungle ravines, and it looks for places like this in English woods. Its reddish brown coat blends with its background, and so you can rarely see it.

The young are born at any time during the summer, and there seems to be no general rutting season.

Muntjacs sometimes utter a loud, barking cry, which is why they are known as Barking Deer. They live in woods in most of the southern counties of England, having spread there since escaping from private collections in parks like Woburn during the past seventy or eighty years.

The Chinese water deer is even smaller than the muntjac; it is seldom more than 16 inches high. Neither the

Left : A muntjac, or barking deer. *Right :* A Chinese water deer.

male nor female has antlers, but the male does have tusks, which are used for fighting.

This deer was brought from China and settled in parks in England, from which quite a few have escaped in the past forty years. It is now fairly widespread in southern England.

This fragile little deer differs from most other deer in that it produces four to six young at a time. These are generally born in May and June. The rutting season is in December and January.

The Chinese water deer is solitary, running alone or in pairs rather than in herds. It skulks in long grass or in bushes and undergrowth of forests, and people rarely see it.

Of the many other kinds of deer which run under almost wild conditions in British parks one of the most interesting is the Père David's Deer. It has a remarkable story.

In the year 1865 a French missionary, Père David, saw a herd of these deer in the grounds of the Chinese Imperial Palace in Peking. He learned that the deer had originally lived in Central Asia but had become extinct there. The herd kept by the Chinese Emperor was the only one in existence.

Eventually the Emperor was persuaded to send some to Paris, and from there some were distributed to other zoos. In England a large herd was built up by the Duke of Bedford, at Woburn. And this was just as well, for not long afterwards there was a revolution in China, and in the confusion all the deer in the Imperial Palace grounds were killed for food. Fortunately those at Woburn had settled down so well that it was possible to use animals from the herd to form new herds elsewhere, including America. And now some have even been sent back to China.

The Père David's deer is a large animal, standing between five and six feet high and weighing up to 500 pounds. It is brownish grey with a few black markings. Its horns are curiously shaped, with one long antler sticking out behind, over its back. Unlike most deer, it has a rather long tail.

Above : A Père David's hind. You can see how unlike European
deer it is. *Below* : A herd of Père David's deer in an English park.

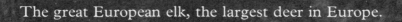
The great European elk, the largest deer in Europe.

7: Deer in Europe and Asia

The largest deer that ever lived was probably the Irish elk, which became extinct long ago. Its near relation, the European elk, is also very large. It sometimes measures seven feet high at the shoulders, and its antlers have a span of over six feet.

It has long legs and can, it is said, run faster than a horse, and keep up the pace for hours. Many years ago it was used to draw sledges in Sweden, but this was made illegal, because so many criminals escaped by using one. Because of its long legs and short neck it has to kneel down to graze.

Usually it lives a solitary life, but in winter, when there is little food, it gathers with other elk. Together they trample on the snow until they have worked through it to the grass and other plants underneath.

The elk is very like the American moose (described in the next chapter), though a little smaller. Its habits are the same. Once it was widespread throughout northern Europe, but now it lives mainly in northern Russia and north Norway. The Russians have partly domesticated

Above : The Kashmir deer of India. *Below :* Axis or spotted deer. They come from India, but some have escaped from parks to live wild in Europe.

the elk, and have half a million or more of them on ranches. They use them for meat, and an elk can produce quite a lot of meat, for it weighs up to 1800 pounds.

The Axis Deer is a very beautiful animal, very similar to the fallow deer but with even more white spots. It will interbreed with the fallow. Although its home is India and Ceylon, it has been introduced to many other countries, where it soon settles down in parks. In New Zealand it has become especially common. Axis deer generally roam through the forest in small herds but sometimes gather together in great herds of several hundred animals.

Other fine deer found in India are the Kashmir Deer and Wallich's Deer, both of which stand over four feet high. Thorold's Deer, which lives in south-western China, is very like the red deer but has a white muzzle.

The Reindeer is different from most other deer, because it likes open country better than forest. It is an animal of the Arctic tundra and is well adapted to life in the harsh conditions there.

Standing about four feet high, the reindeer is about the same size as the red deer. It has very large, flattened hooves, which enable it to walk on snow. It grows a thick and soft fur coat, which is grey in summer and almost white in winter. Its antlers are long and spreading, and females as well as males have them.

Reindeer live on mosses and lichen, scraping away the snow with their hooves in winter. Hardly any reindeer

In Russia government officials used to use reindeer to tow their sleighs when they went out on business.

now exist in the wild; they are all domesticated. In Lapland and northern Siberia great herds provide most of the things that are needed by the human inhabitants. They supply milk and meat. Their hides make good leather. They are trained to draw sledges and to carry packs on their backs.

Reindeer were once found much farther south in Europe. It is said that they were hunted in northern Scotland until about eight hundred years ago. In 1952 a herd was set up on the Cairngorm mountains and is now about a hundred strong. Reindeer have also been taken to the Canadian Arctic and to Alaska, where they have settled down happily.

8 : American Deer

There is a great variety of deer in the Americas. The American Wapiti is almost exactly the same as the European red deer though larger. In America it is sometimes called the elk. It stands over five feet high and weighs up to 900 pounds.

The animal most resembling the European elk in America is known as the Moose. It is a magnificent animal, – easily the largest living deer. Large moose can stand nearly eight feet high and weigh almost 2000 pounds. The males have huge antlers, spreading and flattened.

Male moose are called *bulls*; females *cows*; and the youngsters *calves*. Twins are quite common among moose; the calves are born in spring and stay with their mothers for about two years.

Moose usually live on their own. They are so large and need so much food that no countryside could support great herds of them. In summer they are fond of water and spend much of their time wading in streams and lakes, eating the plants and greenery that they find. In winter they browse on twigs and paw aside the snow to get at the

A herd of wapiti in a Canadian national park. In North America they are often known as elk.

green underneath. The moose has a long, rubbery lip which helps it to grasp and tear off twigs almost out of its reach. It also uses its great weight to secure food, sometimes leaning against a young tree until it falls down, so that it can get at the twigs.

Mating takes place in September, when the male moose's antlers are at their best. The bull and cow moose bellow loudly to each other across the autumn woods. Indian hunters used to use a birch bark trumpet to imitate the moose's bellow and so lure the animal within range of their arrows or guns.

The North American animal most like the reindeer is the Caribou, a splendid animal whose picture is on the

The largest deer in the world—the moose. *Above :* An enormous bull moose. *Below :* A cow moose and calf.

postage stamps of Newfoundland. Like the reindeer, it has a thick, woolly coat and large, flattened hooves to walk on snow. Both males and females have antlers, though the female's are much smaller than the male's.

There are two kinds of caribou. The *Woodland Caribou* live in the forests of northern Canada and do not form large herds. The *Barren Ground Caribou* live on the treeless tundra all the summer, feeding on the plentiful vegetation which grows there. In autumn the barren ground caribou migrate southwards to the forests. On these migrations they assemble in enormous herds, sometimes of 20,000 to 30,000. The journey may be as long as 700 miles, and on the way the caribou are at-

A herd of caribou on the move.

tacked by wolves, Indians and Eskimoes, while foxes, hawks and ravens linger around to pick up stray titbits after a kill. In recent years the numbers of caribou have declined, mainly because of forest fires in their winter quarters. As a result, the Indian and Eskimo tribes which relied on them for food have suffered great hardship.

The name *Caribou* is an Indian one, meaning *the shoveller*. It refers to the caribou's habit of shovelling the snow with its broad hooves, in order to get at the lichens and other vegetation beneath. It is also said to use its horns for the same purpose.

The most numerous of all deer in North America is the White-tailed Deer, or Virginian Deer. It is rather

63

smaller than the red deer. It lives on the edge of woods, from which it can move out into meadow or cultivated country. Although hunters shoot at it a lot it is flourishing and is increasing in numbers. It can run very fast, up to 40 miles per hour, can jump an eight-foot fence and is always on the alert. When alarmed it raises its tail, showing its white tail patch as a warning to its companions. It does not gather in large herds but travels through the woods in small family parties.

In the western parts of the United States of America the commonest deer is the Mule Deer. This animal is a little smaller than the white-tailed deer. It spends much of its time in woodlands but likes to come out to feed on grassy plains. It is one of the deer which forms large herds. In autumn these migrate from the mountains, where the deer spend the summer, to sheltered valleys. Mating takes place in November, and each male forms a harem.

South America has its own kinds of deer. One is the tiny Pudu, which stands only fifteen inches high and is the smallest deer in the world. It lives in Chile. The Guemal is a medium-sized deer with short antlers which lives in mountain areas. The Pampas Deer, which is much like the roe deer, is an animal of the plains, or pampas. Another small deer is the Brocket, which lives in dense tropical forests. The Marsh Deer is another forest deer, which likes marshy country and the banks of rivers. It is the same size as the red deer and has fine antlers.

Two of the commonest deer in the United States. *Right:* A white-tailed buck. *Below:* A mule deer in Yellowstone National Park.

9: Deer in the Tropics

In Africa there are no deer. They have antelopes instead. Tropical Asia, however, has many deer. They are of two types. There are the large deer with antlers, that live in forests and on grassy plains. And there are the small deer, like roe deer, which creep about in the thickest parts of the forest.

Typical of the large deer are the Sambar Deer of India and Indo-China. They are larger than the red deer and weigh up to 700 pounds, but have rather small antlers. They live in dense woodlands in hilly districts and generally come out to feed only at night. They form in small herds.

The Barasingha is not quite as large. It too lives in India, but on the edge of forests rather than in them. When the mating season begins the barasinghas gather in herds of forty or fifty, but when the young are born and the stags are growing new antlers the herds break up. When left to themselves the barasinghas come out to graze by day, but they have been so badly persecuted by hunters that they now only appear at night. They are also known as Swamp Deer, because they like water so much.

A sambar stag, from India. Indian deer are hunted so much that now they come out only at night.

Of the smaller deer the muntjacs, already mentioned (on page 50), are typical. There are both Indian and Chinese muntjacs. A similar animal is the Musk Deer, which has a special gland containing musk. This is very precious in the East, for mixing perfumes and medicines. As a result, the unfortunate musk deer has been harried and shot until it is now very rare. The musk deer lives in wooded mountain regions on the borders of India and

The head of the little musk deer of Central Asia. It has sharp teeth instead of antlers, and is valued by traders for the scent gland on its stomach.

China. It has no antlers, but two of its teeth are developed into sharp tusks.

In the dense forests of Malaysia and Indonesia live some tiny deer called Mouse Deer or Chevrotains. Because they spend their lives creeping about in the thick undergrowth near tropical streams they have no antlers, which could become entangled in branches. There are many kinds of mouse deer, but all are about eighteen inches high. They are timid, furtive creatures, which come out to feed at night and seldom go far from water, into which they dive as soon as they are alarmed.

10: Deer and Man

Like all plant-eating animals, deer are preyed on by *carnivores* or flesh-eating animals. In northern countries their chief enemies are wolves, lynxes and, for the young animals, foxes and eagles. In the tropics they are tigers, leopards, jaguars and smaller wild cats.

In Britain and most other West European countries carnivorous animals large enough to prey on deer have been killed off long ago. The deer's only real enemy is mankind.

Deer hunting. The dogs have chased this frightened doe into the freezing cold river . . .

Because deer do great damage to farmers and foresters, by eating trees and all kinds of cultivated crops, they would all have been killed long before now – if it were not for the sport they give to other men. So men destroy *and* men protect deer.

In Britain people hunt deer in two different ways. In southern England they are hunted with hounds, known as staghounds or buckhounds. The hounds hunt in a pack, pick up the scent of a deer and follow it. Huntsmen on horses and wearing special uniform accompany them. Similar hunts take place in much of Europe, where dogs known as elkhounds are also employed.

On the Scottish moors and mountains the deer are killed by stalking. Men with high-powered rifles spend days on the bleak mountains, trying to creep near enough to a deer to get a shot at it. Generally only one sportsman goes out on a stalking expedition, accompanied by a keeper or guide and a pony to carry the dead deer home.

In the Middle Ages, when kings and nobles reserved the deer for themselves, it was rather different. The hunters stood hidden in bushes along the edge of a wood, and keepers drove the deer towards them. When the deer came within range, the waiting sportsmen shot them with arrows.

In most European countries there is what is called a *close season*, during which deer may not be legally hunted

Right: . . . but the doe manages to scramble out on to the snowy bank . . .

or shot. Some countries allow shooting only on licence. In some states in America, however, a man who has a gun licence can kill as many deer as he likes. In the state of Oregon alone over 160,000 mule deer were shot by hunters in one recent year. In India deer have been so persecuted by hunters that some kinds have survived only by hiding in the deepest jungles or in impassable swamps.

Although deer are killed mainly for sport, their flesh is usually not wasted but eaten. The meat is known as *venison*. It is dark and rather strong but some people like it very much.

Reindeer are deer that have been partly domesticated. Some of them are tame enough to be milked, like cows, and even those which appear to be wild have marks in their ears to show whose they are. Herdsmen from Lapland have been taken to northern Canada to teach the Eskimoes there how to herd caribou. The Russians, too, have taken up reindeer herding.

Wildlife in India and the tropics is threatened, and the deer which live there share the danger of extinction. Once an animal is extinct it is gone for ever: there is no getting it back. But in northern and western countries deer have fewer attackers and they are more protected than ever before; so in these parts at least their future looks bright. Hopefully many kinds of deer will be with us for all time.

. . . and quickly disappears into the trees, safe once more.

Glossary

ANTLERS. The branched horns of deer. Usually carried by the males only but by females as well in a few species, such as the reindeer and caribou.

BARE BUCK. A male fallow deer, four to five years old.

BELLING. The roaring sound made by a male red deer in the mating season.

BROCKET. A male red deer in its second year.

BUCK. A male fallow or roe deer. It refers particularly to a male fallow deer in its sixth and seventh year.

CALF. A young red deer.

CAMOUFLAGE. Concealment by blending with one's background. It is usually achieved in nature by a colour pattern which breaks up the outline of the animal as well as matching the background. The animal must also remain perfectly still.

CARNIVORES. Flesh-eating animals.

COW. A female red deer or moose.

DELAYED IMPLANTATION. A peculiar arrangement, found in the roe deer, whereby the foetus or young deer does not start to grow within the body of its mother until several months after fertilization.

DOE. A female deer (though not of the red deer or moose, whose females are known as cows).

FAWN. The young of most deer, though not of red deer or moose.

GESTATION PERIOD. The period between mating and the birth of a baby animal; the period during which the baby is carried in its mother's body.

GREAT BUCK. A fully-grown male fallow deer, usually at eight years and over.

HAREM. A collection of wives, as acquired by male deer of many species.

HERBIVOROUS. A term applied to animals which eat only plants.

HIND. Female red deer.

HUMMEL. A male red deer which fails to grow antlers; it is often bigger and heavier than other stags.

KNOBBER. A male red deer calf before he grows his antlers.

NOCTURNAL. A nocturnal animal is one which is active at night.

POLYGAMOUS. A male animal which usually has more than one wife.

PRICKET. A young male fallow deer when it has grown its first set of antlers.

RUMINANT. An animal which chews the cud; it eats its food quickly and passes it into its first stomach, then, when resting later, brings it back into its mouth, chews it and passes it for digestion into another stomach.

RUTTING SEASON. The mating season for deer.

SORE. A male fallow deer in its fourth year.

SOREL. A male fallow deer in its third year.

SPAYAD. A male red deer in its third year.

STAG. An adult male red deer.

STAG ROYAL. A large mature stag with twelve or more points to its antlers.

STAGGARD. A male red deer in its fourth year.

STALKING. The sport of shooting deer by creeping up stealthily and quietly to within rifle range.

TERRITORY. An area of land regarded by an animal as its own property. In the mating season a male deer will have a territory which it marks by rubbing various glands of its body against bushes, trees or rocks; and it will fight any other male which ventures on this territory.

TUNDRA. Treeless land, covered with moss, lichens and other small plants in summer and frozen hard in winter, on the edge of the Arctic Ocean.

VENISON. Deermeat.

Finding Out More

Books to read:

The Book of the British Countryside (Automobile Association).

The Fallow Deer (Forestry Commission Leaflet, H.M.S.O.).

The Living World of Animals (Readers Digest Association).

Michael Blackmore, *Mammals in Britain* (Collins).

Maurice Burton, *Systematic Dictionary of Mammals of the World* (Museum Press).

F. Fraser Darling, *Natural History in the Highlands and Islands* (Collins).

H. L. Edlin, *Wild Life of Wood and Forest* (Hutchinson).

Norman E. Hickin, *The Natural History of an English Forest* (Arrow).

Alan C. Jenkins, *Wild Life in Danger* (Methuen).

M. J. Lawrence and R. W. Brown, *Mammals of Britain: their Tracks, Trails and Signs* (Blandford).

L. Harrison Matthews, *British Mammals* (Collins).

Marion Nixon, *The Oxford Book of Vertebrates* (Oxford U.P.).

F. J. T. Page, *A Field Guide to British Deer* (Blackwell).

Balakrishna Seshadri, *The Twilight of India's Wild Life*
(John Baker).

Places to visit:

You can see *Red Deer* on Exmoor and a few other places in Devon and Somerset; also in the Lake District. They are numerous in the Scottish Highlands. There are also a few in the New Forest and in many parks, including Richmond Park.

Fallow Deer and *Roe Deer* may be seen in and around woods in most parts of southern England. Roe deer are also quite plentiful in Scotland, but fallow deer are scarcer there and in Wales.

Muntjacs and *Chinese Water Deer* live wild in some woodland districts in the Midlands, having escaped from or having been set free in certain parks, notably Woburn. The *Sika* is rather more widely distributed.

It must be remembered that most deer hide themselves, in woodland or tall fern, during the day and come out to feed only in the late evening. In parks and zoological gardens, however, they sit chewing their cud in open grassland by day, and so you can easily watch them.

Reindeer exist in Britain only in one herd on the tops of the Cairngorm Mountains.

The Council for Nature, Zoological Gardens, Regent's Park, London NW1 4RY, is a clearing house for information about animals in Britain.

Index

Picture Credits

The author and publishers thank the following for permission to reproduce copyright illustrations: Frank W. Lane, *frontispiece*, pp. 9, 11 (below), 12, 14, 16, 22, 25, 29, 30–1, 32, 33, 34, 35, 38–9, 43, 51 (right), 54, 60, 61, 62–3, 65; Mary Evans Picture Library, *title page*; Bruce Coleman Ltd, pp. 6, 20; Heather Angel, pp. 8 (left), 11 (above), 37, 38, 39, 53 (above); Blandford Press, pp. 8 (right), 19; Paul Popper Ltd, pp. 13, 15, 21, 23, 27, 51 (left), 56 (above), 58, 67, 68; Natural History Photographic Agency, pp. 18, 41, 45, 46, 49, 53 (below), 56 (below); Ardea Photographics, pp. 44, 47; Keystone Press Agency Ltd, pp. 69, 71, 73.